OUR FATHERS, SONS, LOVERS AND LITTLE BROTHERS

OUR FATHERS, SONS, LOVERS AND LITTLE BROTHERS

MAKAMBE K SIMAMBA

PLAYWRIGHTS CANADA PRESS
TORONTO

LIBRARY AND ARCHIVES CANADA CATALOGUING IN PUBLICATION
Title: Our fathers, sons, lovers and little brothers / Makambe K. Simamba.
Names: Simamba, Makambe K., author.
Description: First edition. | A play.
Identifiers: Canadiana (print) 20210250127 | Canadiana (ebook) 20210250135
| ISBN 9780369102423 (softcover) | ISBN 9780369102430 (PDF)
| ISBN 9780369102447 (HTML)
Classification: LCC PS8637.I3645 O97 2021 | DDC C812/.6—dc23

Playwrights Canada Press operates on Mississaugas of the Credit, Wendat, Anishinaabe, Métis, and Haudenosaunee land. It always was and always will be Indigenous land.

We acknowledge the financial support of the Canada Council for the Arts, the Ontario Arts Council (OAC), Ontario Creates, and the Government of Canada for our publishing activities.

Canada Council for the Arts | Conseil des arts du Canada

For the Simamba men

Our Fathers, Sons, Lovers and Little Brothers was first produced by b current performing arts at Buddies in Bad Times Theatre, Toronto, from April 11 to 18, 2019, with the following cast and creative team:

Written and performed by Makambe K Simamba

Director: Donna-Michelle St. Bernard
Dramaturge: Audrey Dwyer
Stage Manager: Dylan Tate-Howarth
Production Manager: Suzie Balogh
Lighting and Projection Design: Trevor Schwellnus
Sound Design: Maddie Bautista
Assistant Sound Design: Diana Reyes
Choreography: Makambe K Simamba
Choreography Consultant: Shakeil Rollock
Marketing and Publicity: Sue Edworthy
Social Amplification and Community Outreach: Dalton Higgins

The play was developed with the support of Alberta Theatre Projects, the Banff Playwrights Lab, and UNO Fest.

If I ruled the world
(Imagine that)
I'd free all my sons

—Nas, "If I Ruled the World (Imagine That)"
ft. Lauryn Hill

CHARACTERS

Slimm

The last inhale.

A seventeen-year-old Black boy in a hoodie appears. His body parts isolate, moving in a way that is unfamiliar.

SLIMM: What just happened?

He considers his own body. He tries to control his limbs.

I'm hot. I'm wet?

He observes the space. He sees eyes watching him.

GOD!?

The Lord is my shepherd; I shall not want.
He makes me lie down in green pastures.
He leads me beside still waters.
He restores my soul.
He leads me in paths of righteousness for his name's sake.
Even though I walk through the valley
of the shadow of death,
I fear no evil,
For you are with me.

He remembers to do the sign of the cross.

(to the eyes) I haven't been to church in a minute. I just thought I'd slip in a little insurance.

Are y'all here for Judgment Day?

Is God on Black people time?

There should be like a step-by-step instruction manual.

A large book appears.

The boy approaches the book.

(reading) "*Your Journey to the Ancestors.*"

The book glows and inscribes itself.

"*A Step-by-Step Instruction Manual.*"

"Open me."

Mmm-mmm.

He walks away from the book.

GRANDMA appears.

GRANDMA: Baby, you stand on the shoulders of the ancestors who chose you to represent them in this moment.

She points at the book.

Open it.

SLIMM: Grandma? Aren't you the one who used to force me to go to church? Where's God? And why do I have to . . .

GRANDMA: That sperm hit that egg and you were no mistake.

SLIMM: Did you just say sperm?

GRANDMA disappears.

Grandma?

SLIMM looks at the book.

God is actually kind of savage.

(to the eyes) Have you read the Old Testament? He turned a bitch into salt just for looking back.

I got another one. God is so savage . . .

You're supposed to say, "How savage is he?"

God is so savage . . .

He waits for "How savage is he?"

Um, okay, so he hollas at his homeboy and tells him to spend like two entire months building this huge-ass fucking boat. Then he makes him scour da whole earff, gatherin' all the animals, like, two of each one and shit just to be like, "I'M GONNA MAKE IT FLOOD," and it's like, "Dude, you had the power to make a flood but you didn't have the power to build your own boat?"

Laughter.

God is so savage . . .

He waits for "How savage is he?"

So it's like a Tuesday morning, like a couple thousand years ago, right? God calls up his friend Abraham, right? And he's like *(to the tune of Lionel Richie)* "Hello . . . is it me you're lookin' for?"

Just kidding, just kidding. That was . . . bad. So he's like, "Hey, Abe. It's me, Lord. Yeah, nigga. What's good? Yeah yeah, okay. How's work? Cool . . . cool. How's your wife? Okay, cool. How's your only son? Great. I'ma need you to sacrifice him."

(hanging up the imaginary phone) Click!

And so Abraham takes his fucking kid, drags this lil nigga up a mountain, puts him down on like a altar or some shit, lifts up this huge-ass rock and just as he's about to smash his head into a thousand tiny pieces, God be like, "JUST KIDDING . . . KIDDING . . . Kidding."

Abraham's just like . . .

SLIMM does some Abraham improv.

Then God didn't say nothin' else.

Savage. Ancestors all the way.

SLIMM opens the book.

"*Your Journey to the Ancestors: A Step-by-Step Instruction Manual.* STEP 1: PERFORM A SACRED CEREMONY TO SANCTIFY THE SPACE."

SLIMM does the Soulja Boy dance. When he's done, his arm floats in the air. SLIMM observes his arm and then slowly shakes it off.

Gravity feels different here.

The book glows. Each sentence in the book appears just before it needs to be read.

"*Your Journey to the Ancestors: A Step-by-Step Instruction Manual.* STEP 2: READ THE FOLLOWING PASSAGE."

"Welcome to the beginning of the rest of your eternity. Your time on Earth has come to an end."

"*By reading this sentence aloud* you solemnly swear that you will swiftly complete all the steps of this instruction manual."

"*By reading this sentence aloud* you agree to trust this manual's every instruction to guide you through this process and agree to all consequences of non-compliance."

"*By reading this sentence aloud* you agree that failure to complete all steps will result in eternal torment and separation from your ancestors."

Can we go back? I feel like there's been a mistake.

"You are not here by mistake. Stubbornness, avoidance and procrastination will not be tolerated. Place one hand on your heart and one hand in the centre of this manual. Swear."

He does.

I swear.

"*Your Journey to the Ancestors: A Step-by-Step Instruction Manual.* STEP 3: INTRODUCE YOURSELF."

(to the eyes) Slimm.

The book doesn't respond.

(to the book) I'm Slimm?

The book doesn't respond.

(to the space) I AM SLIMM!

The book glows.

"*Your Journey to the Ancestors: A Step-by-Step Instruction Manual.* STEP 4: TELL THOSE WATCHING ABOUT YOURSELF."

Uh so, yeah, people call me Slimm. I'm from Miami. I'm seventeen. This is awkward . . .

The book doesn't respond.

I like football and basketball?

The book doesn't respond. SLIMM *walks away from the book.*

My favourite rappers are Tupac, then DMX, then Mystikal . . . in that order.

SLIMM *quickly turns toward the book to see if the book has accepted his answer.*

The book doesn't respond.

I like Krispy Kreme doughnuts . . . and Sour Patch Kids? And Fruit Roll-Ups. And 7-Eleven one-dollar hot dogs. And Cool Ranch Doritos. And anything from Bob's Wings and Grill. Just food—I like food in general.

Flashback: SLIMM, *seventeen, and his mother,* SYBRINA, *in their living room in Miami. It's the day before.*

SYBRINA: This is not the way I raised you! You do not lie, you do not steal, you do not do graffiti and you do not under any circumstances skip school!

Where is your head? So now you don't care about college?

SLIMM: I still wanna go.

SYBRINA: And you think you'll get in at this rate? When the school is calling, telling me you have marijuana in your bag and that you've skipped class three times this week?

SLIMM: Are you gonna ground me?

SYBRINA looks away in frustration.

SYBRINA: I am sick and tired of grounding you.

SLIMM: You kickin' me out?

SYBRINA: You gonna keep acting like a bad kid?

SLIMM: I'm not a bad kid. Mom! Where am I supposed to go?

SYBRINA: You have ten days off of school to think about what you've done, but you're not gonna be sitting around my house. There's a 3:30 bus to Sanford. Your father can deal with you when you get there.

Another flashback: outside SYBRINA's house. DENNIS approaches.

DENNIS: Yo, Slimm. See you later at my place for the All-Star Game?

SLIMM: Remind me never to get high with you in the middle of school ever again.

DENNIS: But it makes those one-dollar hot dogs and the Cool Ranch Doritos taste better . . . Oh shit.

SLIMM: Wack-ass vice principal caught me in the hall while I was trying to go to Chemistry.

DENNIS: *(holding in his laughter)* So right after I turned the corner?

SLIMM: My bag was open. Ten-day suspension.

DENNIS: Oo, nigga, that's stress.

SLIMM: My mom lost it.

DENNIS: There's worse things than weed.

SLIMM: But like she wasn't even that mad about the weed? It was all about "How could you skip class," "What are your goals," "No son of mine," blah blah blah.

Know what the fucked-up part is? Of all the classes I skipped today, I actually wanted to go to Chemistry.

DENNIS: Don't worry. I'm sure Rachel will give you some of her notes . . . And probably a little something extra.

SLIMM: D. I'm not in the mood.

DENNIS: My bad, nigga.

SLIMM: I gotta go to my dad's.

DENNIS: Aight. See you when you get back?

End of flashback. SLIMM's arms drop and he is out of breath, shocked from the experience. His right arm floats up. He doesn't notice it at first, but when he sees it, he grabs it and holds it in place.

The book glows and begins to write.

SLIMM: "*Your Journey to the Ancestors: A Step-by-Step Instruction Manual.* STEP 5: TAKE THIS TIME TO HAVE A MOMENT TO YOURSELF."

SLIMM takes a moment to himself. There is an uncomfortable intake and outtake of breath to try and process his surroundings. He approaches the book. He clears his throat.

"*Your Journey to the Ancestors: A Step-by-Step Instruction Manual.* STEP 6: THINK OF YOUR LOVED ONES AND SEND THEM A SIGN TO LET THEM KNOW YOU'RE OKAY."

(angry, controlled) That's it? That's all I get??

I don't know if friends count as loved ones, but . . . obviously Rachel. Dennis. All my friends from school and the block. My football coach. My camp instructors.

Auntie Geraldine.

Brandi. Mom . . .

Flashback: SLIMM*'s father,* TRACY, *and his sons are in the car.* JAHVARIS, *fifteen, is driving.* SLIMM *is eleven.* CHAD *is three.* CHAD *has his thumb in his mouth.*

TRACY *gestures driving directions to* JAHVARIS. *A strong silence, and then . . .*

TRACY: At one point, *you're* gonna be the one driving and a police officer is gonna pull you over. Cause they can. So they will. When that happens, what are you gonna do, hm? What did you see Jahvaris do?

SLIMM: Stay calm?

TRACY: And what else?

SLIMM *looks at* JAHVARIS.

JAHVARIS: You always gotta call them sir.

SLIMM: Why?

TRACY: Because the world is a scary place for a Black man and you need to do whatever I tell you.

Jahvaris. Turn here, get back on the highway.

JAHVARIS: Where are we going?

TRACY: Home. I need to fix the brake light.

SLIMM: I thought you said we was going to the movies.

JAHVARIS: Slimm. Chill.

SLIMM: But, Dad, you promised. You promised that you was gonna take me and Jahvaris and Chad to the movies.

TRACY: I said NO.

CHAD starts to fuss.

You're making your little brother upset.

Jahvaris, pull the car over. I need to drive.

JAHVARIS pulls over. JAHVARIS and TRACY switch seats.

And another thing. Always keep your hands on the steering wheel—where they can see them. Which you did. Remember, next time, when you have to reach into your pocket to grab your licence, *ask them* if it's okay first.

JAHVARIS: Okay, Dad. I will.

TRACY: Before your grandma died, she always told me: if anybody comes at you with any type of racism, confrontation isn't worth it. Do not discuss it because confrontation may escalate. If you have to defend yourself, do so. But if you can, just run.

SLIMM: But last week you grounded me because you said I was having a bad attitude and you said that if I have a bad attitude then I'm gonna keep finding reasons to have a bad attitude . . . so if you just feel scared all the time aren't you just gonna keep finding more reasons to be scared all the time? Dad?! He didn't even give us a ticket, and how come this means we can't go to the movies?

TRACY: END OF DISCUSSION.

CHAD cries big tears. TRACY carefully puts on his seat belt, checks his mirrors, flicks on the turn signal, shoulder checks and begins to drive.

SLIMM puts his arm around CHAD.

SLIMM: Don't cry, Chad.

SLIMM glares at his dad.

End of flashback.

And send a sign to Dad. Jahvaris. And especially Chad.

SLIMM does a physical gesture that makes sense to him to send them a sign. Then he puts his hands in the sleeves of his hoodie and shifts uncomfortably.

"*Your Journey to the Ancestors: A Step by Step Instruction Manual.* STEP 7: YOU WILL FIND A POUCH CONTAINING SAND, SOIL AND GRASS BLESSED BY YOUR ANCESTORS."

A pouch appears.

"SPRINKLE IT AROUND YOURSELF. THIS STEP COMPLETES THE RELEASE OF YOUR PHYSICAL BODY'S LAST BREATH."

I won't!

SLIMM throws the pouch across the room and is immediately thrown into a flashback.

Flashback: SLIMM and DENNIS outside their high school days before. SLIMM holds a joint.

Man, Dennis. My mom and dad are *tripping* 'bout "I haven't been focusing on my studies." I told my mom, "Bs and Cs are not that bad," and she was like, "If you can do better, then okay is not enough."

I look at it like this:

SLIMM takes a drag.

Why do you even go to school? It's so that you can learn to read and write. And then they're just gearing you up to figure out what career you wanna have. Okay, perfect. I already know what I'm gonna be, so what's the point? Nah, for real, why I gotta be struggling in like, English, and Social Studies, when I already know what's good?

SLIMM passes the joint to DENNIS.

DENNIS: At least she cares.

SLIMM: Sometimes I think she cares too much.

DENNIS holds his breath, and then exhales.

DENNIS: You know, you ain't really helping yourself by getting high in the middle of the school day.

DENNIS passes the joint back to SLIMM.

SLIMM: *(inhaling smoke)* A man's gotta do what a man's gotta do.

They laugh. SLIMM coughs.

DENNIS: But your dad—

DENNIS takes the joint from SLIMM.

He doesn't live with you, but he still checks for you, right? And your mom, she's trippin', but at least she cares.

SLIMM: What, you wanna take my parents off my hands? What is this, 1-800-Adopt-A-Nigga?

SLIMM elbows DENNIS. DENNIS reacts by stepping his right foot back.

DENNIS: No, I don't wanna take them off your hands. I'm just saying, not everybody has that.

DENNIS takes his final drag, drops the roach on the floor and steps on it.

So what you gonna be then, Slimm? When you finish school? Since you've got it all figured out.

SLIMM: You mean other than a bona fide hustla?

Beat.

Flashback: TRACY is dropping SLIMM back at SYBRINA's house. SLIMM is fourteen. SYBRINA is mixing something in a bowl.

TRACY: Guess who was mentoring some of the younger kids this week.

SYBRINA: Is that right?

(to SLIMM) What was your favourite part, your favourite part of the whole flight camp?

SLIMM: When we got to fly.

SYBRINA: You got to fly?

SLIMM: Mom, they put that on the brochure. You already knew that.

SYBRINA: *(putting her bowl down)* Well, why aren't you more excited about it?

SLIMM is silent.

TRACY: You're gonna tell the whole camp you wanna be a pilot but you won't tell your own mother?

SLIMM puts his hands in the sleeves of his hoodie.

SLIMM: It's expensive . . .

TRACY: Remember what we talked about? Don't worry about things you don't need to be worrying about. I'm proud of you. Love you. See you next weekend.

TRACY kisses SLIMM on the cheek and exits. SLIMM wipes the kiss off of his cheek and waves at his dad.

SYBRINA: You hungry, Pilot Martin? Mh. Don't you like the way that sounds? Just think, clouds rushing past you on either side. My son, piercing through the sky at six hundred miles per hour.

SLIMM smiles shyly.

Alright, Mr. Pilot. Where you gonna take me?

SLIMM: Atlanta.

SYBRINA: You gonna take me to somewhere I could drive to? Please.

SLIMM: California.

SYBRINA: I've already been there.

SLIMM: Where do you wanna go?

SYBRINA: You tell me.

SLIMM: Italy! You could ride on a gondola, and they got really good pizza.

SYBRINA: You like food too much. What else you got?

SLIMM: Australia? To see the Great Barrier Reef?

SYBRINA contemplates.

How 'bout the Carnival . . . in . . . BRAZIL!?

SYBRINA: Hm.

SLIMM: South Africa? China. Ecuador? Norway! I don't know, Mom. The world is huge!

SYBRINA: Exactly. And you're gonna fly all over it.

Beat.

SLIMM: You really think I can do it?

SYBRINA: You really think you can't?

End of flashback.

SLIMM: "*Your Journey to the Ancestors: A Step-by-Step Instruction Manual.* STEP 7 REVISED: COVER YOUR EYES WITH YOUR HANDS AND INHALE TO LIVE THROUGH YOUR LAST MOMENTS. THEN FIND THE POUCH CONTAINING SAND, SOIL AND GRASS BLESSED BY YOUR ANCESTORS. SPRINKLE IT AROUND YOURSELF TO RELEASE YOUR PHYSICAL BODY'S LAST BREATH."

You want—you want me to be face to face with that chump again? You want him to call me a nigger again and tell me I'm up to no good?

That is the stupidest fucking shit I have ever heard and I'm not doing it.

Why am *I* here? I didn't do anything wrong!

Flashback, but this one is different: SLIMM *is fourteen and* JAHVARIS *is eighteen.* JAHVARIS *is playing Xbox. The book glows and shakes.*

JAHVARIS: When a police officer stops you, make sure you stay calm.

SLIMM: Jahvaris.

JAHVARIS: When a police officer stops you, make sure you always call him sir.

SLIMM: I do.

JAHVARIS: Don't escalate the situation.

SLIMM: I don't.

JAHVARIS: Make sure your hands are where he can see them.

SLIMM: You sound like Dad.

SLIMM realizes that something is off. The world of the flashback has begun to blur into the world of the afterlife.

VOICE: When a police officer stops you, don't run.

SLIMM snaps himself out of the flashback.

SLIMM: *(to the book)* What if it's not a police officer?!

SLIMM sees TRACY enter. CHAD, nine, is watching TV.

TRACY: Big man Chad.

CHAD: Hi, Daddy.

TRACY: Where's your brother?

CHAD: *(smiling, bouncy)* He went to get me Skittlesssss!

SLIMM is back in the space. The book makes a can of watermelon AriZona iced tea appear. SLIMM defiantly drinks the iced tea, but the book won't let him swallow and the iced tea wets SLIMM's hoodie.

SLIMM: *(casually)* That shit'll rot your teeth anyway.

SLIMM sees three Skittles roll across the space. As he crosses to pick them up, the book makes a wave of Skittles crash at SLIMM's feet.

MOM!

He opens his eyes and searches for his mother's face in the crowd.

DADDY???

He covers his eyes with his hands and weeps. A big inhale. The book glows.

The Skittles begin to disappear as the room starts to look like a street. Street lamps pop out of the floor. A sidewalk emerges beneath him.

The Lord is my shepherd; I shall not want.
He makes me lie down in green pastures.
He leads me beside still waters.
He restores my soul . . .

SLIMM is now in Sanford. His phone rings.

Rachel!

SLIMM does the happy dance he always does when Rachel calls. He answers like a cool guy.

What's good? Yeah. I was just at the 7-Eleven . . . No, I'm staying at my dad's . . . I'm still gonna watch the game. I just . . . My brother wanted Skittles.

Sanford.

For real? I think you'd like it. The downtown is cool, it's like right on a lake. And there's like little shops and stuff.

Like twenty minutes, walking. Hold on one sec.

He scrolls through his phone briefly. He punches a code into the keypad at the gate.

Sorry. I forgot the code to the gate.

He laughs softly.

Yeah.

I wish you were here too.

I see . . . my feet?

Okay. I see sand, I see soil, I see grass, I see pavement . . . I see the gate closing. Like that?

Okay. I see . . . a pond. I see the swimming pool. I see hibiscus flowers. I see the gym. I see a white dude sitting in his car. I see yellow townhouses everywhere. I see my dad's front door. I see a bike. I see mailboxes.

He stops at the mailboxes.

Is it raining over by you? Yeah, but it's not too bad. You're cute.

He puts on his hood and continues to walk.

Alright, your turn, tell me what you see.

SLIMM looks over his shoulder.

What colour?

SLIMM looks over his shoulder.

I think that guy is following me.

Yeah.

Girl, I'm not gonna run. I didn't do anything wrong. I live here.

What, you worrying about me now? I worry about you.

Hold on . . .

SLIMM runs, but the stranger in the car cuts in front of him, stopping him in his tracks. The stranger gets out of the car and approaches.

Why you followin' me?

The stranger attacks SLIMM, who punches him and fights back. SLIMM is eventually pushed to the ground.

HELP!! HELP ME!!

SLIMM continues to fight back. The stranger shoots him in the chest. SLIMM's body releases into the grass as he dies.

Back in the afterlife, SLIMM is paralyzed for a moment. The book makes SLIMM's phone ring. Then it makes his body stand up and pull the phone out of his pocket. SLIMM looks at the phone in shock as his body involuntarily does the Rachel dance.

Rachel?

He realizes what the book is about to make him relive. SLIMM tries to throw the phone but it is stuck to his hands. One by one, his fingers individually grip the phone.

(to the book) Don't make me live it again!

The book glows and produces a pouch in SLIMM's other hand. The pouch glows and SLIMM looks back and forth between each hand.

Fine, I'll do it! I'll do it.

The ringtone stops.

But *only* if I get to send my loved ones a sign and say goodbye properly.

The book glows in agreement and allows SLIMM *to release his phone.*

SLIMM *does a sincere physical gesture that makes sense to him, signifying the beginning of his goodbyes.*

Jahvaris. Thanks for always lookin' out for me. Not only did you teach me how to do so many things, you taught me how to do them thoughtfully, and not everyone is like that. Thanks for being patient with me. You're the best big brother I ever could have asked for and I'm gonna miss you a whole lot.

Dennis—stay cool, nigga.

Rachel. I'm really sorry I won't be able to take you to the prom. I know you really wanted to go, so, if you wanna go with someone else, I won't be mad.

Dad? Every time we talk, on the phone or even in person, before you say bye you always say I love you, and I'm really sorry that I never say it back, especially this last time. I love you too, Dad.

Mom. I'm sorry that I skipped class and smoked weed and spray-painted on the door, and that I got high at school. I knew you wouldn't like those things, but I did them anyway. I'm sorry I got myself sent to Sanford. I wasn't trying to be up to no good. And I'm not a bad kid. I'm your kid. I'm sorry. And I'm gonna miss you, cupcake.

Raindrops begin to fall from above. SLIMM *feels the rain.*

Please don't cry. Mom. I'm okay! I'm gonna be just fine. It only hurt for like a second and then I didn't feel anything—look. I'm okay. I promise.

You and Daddy—you're both always strong for me so now I'm gonna be strong for you. I'm okay—I'm still me. I promise.

The rain lessens.

I promise.

SLIMM *takes a packet of Skittles out of his pocket and gets down on one knee.*

Chad.

I hope that you don't ever forget me, man. And what I need you to know is that it's not your fault and I'm gonna be watching over you for the rest of your life.

SLIMM *kisses the Skittles and lays the package tenderly on the ground. Then he steps away from the Skittles and opens the pouch. The book glows.*

"*Your Journey to the Ancestors: A Step-by-Step Instruction Manual.* STEP 8: SPEAK ONE THING TO THE SPIRIT OF YOUR KILLER."

SLIMM steps away from the book.

The biggest mistake you ever made was thinking that nobody cared about me.

A looseness overcomes SLIMM's body.

"*Your Journey to the Ancestors: A Step-by-Step Instruction Manual.* STEP 9: SUMMON THE ANCESTORS WHO CHOSE YOU BY SPEAKING THEIR NAMES."

SLIMM speaks his ancestors' names, each one becoming a light in the sky.

Daniel Simmons, aged seventy-four, killed 2015
Lamar Smith, sixty-three, 1955
Walter Scott, fifty, 2015
Lieutenant Colonel Lemuel Augustus Penn, forty-eight, 1964
Harry Tyson Moore, forty-six, 1951
Bony Jean-Pierre, forty-six, 2016
George Floyd Jr., forty-six, 2020
Andrew Loku, forty-five, 2015
Eric Garner, forty-three, 2014
Sam DuBose, forty-three, 2015
Keith Lamont Scott, forty-three, 2016
Robert Lawrence White, forty-one, 2018

Elmore Bolling, thirty-nine, 1947
Martin Luther King Jr., thirty-nine, 1968
Tony McDade, thirty-eight, 2020
Medgar Evers, thirty-seven, 1963
Alton Sterling, thirty-seven, 2016
Wharlest Jackson, thirty-six, 1967
Jerame Reid, thirty-six, 2014
Judge Edward Aaron, thirty-four, 1957
Philando Castile, thirty-two, 2016
Tommy Yancy Jr., thirty-two, 2014

George W. Dorsey, twenty-eight, 1946
Akai Gurley, twenty-eight, 2014
Botham Shem Jean, twenty-six, 2018
Jemel Roberson, twenty-six, 2018
Jordan Baker, twenty-six, 2014
D'Andre Campbell, twenty-six, 2020
Freddie Gray, twenty-five, 2015
Ezell Ford, twenty-five, 2014
Michael Stewart, twenty-five, 1983
Ahmaud Arbrey, twenty-five, 2020
Jamar Clark, twenty-four, 2015
Dayne Jones, twenty-four, 2018
Roger Malcolm, twenty-four, 1946
Jonathan Ferrell, twenty-four, 1988
Samuel Thomas Wilkes, twenty-four, 1899
Willie Edwards, twenty-four, 1957

Rufus Lesseur, twenty-three, 1904
Amadou Diallo, twenty-three, 1999
Sean Bell, twenty-three, 2006
Amos Miller, twenty-three, 1888
DeAndre Ballard, twenty-three, 2018
Claude Neal, twenty-three, 1934
Mack Charles Parker, twenty-three, 1959
Kalief Browder, twenty-two, 2015
Mark Clark, twenty-two, 1969
Oscar Grant, twenty-two, 2009
John Crawford III, twenty-two, 2014
Fred Hampton, twenty-one, 1969
James Earl Chaney, twenty-one, 1964
Ron Settles, twenty-one, 1981
Emantic Fitzgerald Bradford Jr., twenty-one, 2018

Tony Terrell Robinson, nineteen, 2015
Michael Donald, nineteen, 1981
Kendrec McDade, nineteen, 2012
Ramarley Graham, eighteen, 2012
VonDerrit Myers Jr., eighteen, 2014
Qusean Whitten, eighteen, 2014
Antonio Martin, eighteen, 2014
Michael Brown, eighteen, 2014

Henry Smith, seventeen, 1893
Laquan McDonald, seventeen, 2014
Edmund Perry, seventeen, 1985
Michael Wade Lawson, seventeen, 1988
Antwon Rose II, seventeen, 2018
Jesse Washington, seventeen, 1916
Kendrick Johnson, seventeen, 2013

Austin Callaway, sixteen, 1940
Otis Parham, sixteen, 1934
Kimani Gray, sixteen, 2013
James Powell, fifteen, 1964
Jordan Edwards, fifteen, 2017
George Stinney Jr., fourteen, 1944
Cameron Tillman, fourteen, 2014
Emmett Till, fourteen, 1955
L.D. Nelson, fourteen, 1911
Jason Smith, fourteen, 2011
Tyre King, thirteen, 2016
Nicholas Heyward Jr., thirteen, 1994
Tamir Rice, twelve, 2014
Clifford Glover, ten, 1973

And all those whose last breaths slipped through pavement and penitentiary, fields and falsity, ships, shores and seas, who have not been named, but who are here, and who matter.

I am Trayvon Benjamin Martin, also known as Slimm, aged seventeen. Killed 2012.

TRAYVON sprinkles the contents of the pouch on the ground around him. The book lights up with the last inscription and TRAYVON doesn't need to look at it because he already knows that it says:

Your Journey to the Ancestors: A Step-by-Step Instruction Manual.
STEP 10: RELEASE.

Movement: TRAYVON joins and embodies his ancestors, both those who came before and after. He sees and embodies images of the universe.

Fishing
Smoking a cigarette
Smoking weed
Pop and locking
Pointing a gun
Rapping
Playing craps
Counting money
Walking in shackles
Playing guitar
Playing drums
Reading a newspaper
Putting his hand in the air
Wiping the sweat off his brow
Holding a newborn baby
Boxing
Planting a flower

Being a flower
Running track
Throwing a football
Hanging from a tree by the neck
The Twist
Taking a bite out of a leg of chicken
Hunting with a bow and arrow
Holding the bars of a prison cell
Panting
High-fiving CHAD
Washing his face
Intimidating someone before a fight
Being kissed on the cheek
Taking Rachel to the prom
The Dougie
Conducting an orchestra
Farming
The perspective of a raindrop

Massaging tired hands
Taking out the garbage
Playing basketball
Cooking
Preaching
Africa
Africa
Africa
The Electric Slide
Playing hopscotch
Hugs
Coaching Little League

Getting down on one knee and proposing
Marching
Texting
Drinking a beverage
Hand-washing clothes
Playing with his hair
Turning on a TV with a remote
The lightness of wind
Playing African drums
Sitting
Sleeping
Praying
Ballet
Voguing
Crawling like a baby
The lightness of wind
Showering
Being tickled
Breathing
Blinking
Anything and everything that is life

He sees, embodies, experiences and understands. He is light. He floats. As he releases, the book disappears.

The last exhale.

Clouds rushing past me on either side. Piercing through the sky at six hundred miles per hour.

Lights.

ACKNOWLEDGEMENTS

While the play is called *Our Fathers, Sons, Lovers and Little Brothers*, I'd like to acknowledge the Black community's Mothers, Daughters, Lovers and Little Sisters, as well as our Parents, Children, Lovers and Younger Siblings. My ancestors guided me to write a piece that focuses on the experience of a straight cis Black male, but it is important to acknowledge that *all* Black lives matter, including those of women, queer folks, trans folks, disabled folks, undocumented folks and folks with records.

I'd like to acknowledge Catherine Hernandez, the powerful ally and arts leader who I have affectionately come to call "Aunty." Catherine is the former artistic director of b current performing arts in Toronto. She saw a reading of this play in its early stages and immediately committed to supporting its development and, against several odds, produced its premiere. Thank you, Aunty.

Thank you to the 2017 Banff Playwrights Lab for giving me the space to safely explore, develop and share the beginnings of this work.

Thank you to Audrey Dwyer for your unparalleled early direction and dramaturgy. You always invited my full intelligence and imagination into our work. This script wouldn't be what it is without you.

Thank you to Donna-Michelle St. Bernard not just for directing the premiere, but for understanding the inner workings of my layered brain and for always being there. Thank you for simply "getting it" and for being a source of guidance, integrity and protection both in the work and in the outside world.

Thank you to my cousin, Ngosa Simbyakula, for driving me four hours from Kansas City, Kansas, to Ferguson, Missouri, for an afternoon because I needed to stand in the place where Michael Brown died. Thank you for telling me that I didn't have to explain why. Thank you to Ngosa's friends Irv, Dre and Jalisha for giving me a tour of Ferguson and sharing what the protests in the wake of Michael Brown's murder looked like, sounded like and felt like.

Thank you to the Legacy Museum and the National Memorial for Peace and Justice in Montgomery, Alabama. There I learned not just stories and names that would become part of the list that concludes the play, I also learned how to place Trayvon's story in the context of Black history. Thank you to these organizations for compiling this information and for creating a much-needed memorial for Black lives lost to white supremacy.

In 2018 I spent a full day researching in Sanford, Florida. As I drove down the street in the early evening, processing what I'd observed and mentally preparing myself for the eight-hour drive back to my motel in Montgomery, a Black man in a white pickup truck waved me down and gestured that I should open my window. When I did, he told me that I'd forgotten to turn my headlights on. My heart skipped a beat. I thanked him sincerely, profusely. He nodded at me before driving ahead. Whoever he is, and wherever he is, thank you to him for looking out for me.

Thank you to my cousin, the late Nchimunya Simamba. This play started as a ten-minute solo performance at the One Yellow Rabbit Summer Lab Intensive in 2016. You passed away in the middle of that intensive. I finished only because I knew you would want me to. I was called to explore the idea of the afterlife because I knew you had just taken your place among our ancestors. Thank you for inspiring and guiding the beginning of this work from the other side.

Thank you to my little brother, Liayo, the reason that Trayvon's story is so important to me. Thank you to my incredible mom, Mwangala, and sister, Ngela, for being consistent sources of love and support.

Thank you to Sybrina Fulton, Tracy Martin and Jahvaris Fulton for your continued integrity and work to keep Trayvon's legacy alive. While Trayvon himself launched the movement, I believe that it is the work of his family that has been instrumental in keeping that movement going. Thank you.

Lastly, thank you to the spirit of Trayvon Benjamin Martin. I never had the privilege of meeting you, Trayvon, but I know that you were more than just a headline. You were a real person. You are sorely missed. *Thank you for awakening us to do better and do more.*

Makambe K Simamba is an award-winning, nationally recognized theatre creator. Her play *Our Fathers, Sons, Lovers and Little Brothers* earned her Dora Mavor Moore Awards for Outstanding New Play and Outstanding Performance in the Theatre for Young Audiences category. Other plays include *A Chitenge Story*, *The Drum Major Instinct*, *MUD* and *Makambe Speaks*. Makambe was the 2020/21 artist-in-residence at Tarragon Theatre. Makambe is proudly Zambian, and her intention is to be of service to her community through her ability to tell stories.

First edition: August 2021
Printed and bound in Canada by Rapido Books, Montreal

Jacket art by Chelsea Charles
Author photo © Lauren Vanderbrook

202-269 Richmond St. W.
Toronto, ON
M5V 1X1

416.703.0013
info@playwrightscanada.com
www.playwrightscanada.com
@playcanpress